*Eelahroo (Long Ago) Nyah (Looking)
Möbö-Möbö (Future)*

Lionel G. Fogarty

Eelahroo (Long Ago)
Nyah (Looking)
Möbö-Möbö
(Future)

Vagabond Press 2014

Acknowledgments: Anton Blank and Kerry Reed Gilbert (eds)
Oranui: Special edition of Maori and Aboriginal Literature.

First published 2014 by Vagabond Press
PO Box 958 Newtown NSW 2042 Australia
www.vagabondpress.net

Eelahroo (Long Ago) Nyah (Looking) Möbö-Möbö (Future)
©Lionel G. Fogarty, 2014.
Cover image © Lionel G. Fogarty

Designed and typeset by Michael Brennan
in Minion Pro 10.5/14

All rights reserved. No part of this publication may be reproduced, stored in a retrieval system or transmitted in any form or by any means electronic, mechanical, photocopying or otherwise without the prior permission of the publisher. The information and views set out in this book are those of the author(s) and do not necessarily reflect the opinion of the publisher.

ISBN 978-1-922181-31-2

CONTENTS

Murgon Brawl Cherbourg Brawls 9
"Daran" "Daran" Forbidden 11
Conservatives Sells 13
Bam Gayandi 16
"Here comes the tranquility incarnation..." 18
Related-Obeying-Aborigines 20
Partner To What Terms 22
Lucky Country Sad Loose Society 24
Maps Gods To Whose 25
Country's Sub's No Suss Towns 26
1967 Encouraged The Right Vote Now? 27
"The fat funny ducking took my woman..." 28
Amplifiers Aims Of Circle 30
Immemorial Conservative 31
Cut An Paste 32
A-U-S-T-R-A-L-I-A- 34
Swift Terrorless 35
Foreign Admiration 37
Literary Embarrassed 39
Perverse Approaches 40
Enrol A Pen Friends 42
Stop The Soap Memories 43
Minds Over Poets 45
Thirty Years From 1983 And Still Growing A
    Tree Roots 48
Metropolis Exertion 53
Register Donate 54
Workshops Needs A Nation's First Hey 56
Olive Pink Fly Over Sums 57

Version Of The Program 58
Travel An Arrive 59
First Nations Australia Writers Workshop 61
Connoisseur 62
"Capital Imaginative" 64
Varuna House 65
Sort Of Sorry 67
Distress Fraying 68
The Country Anywhere Race On Races 69
Advance Those Asian And Pacific Writers Poets 70
Journal Version 75
Encounters Conflicts 76
Gallery Mansions Murders 77
A Glance 78
Condensation A Piercings 79
By A Virgin Man 80
Disburse My Voice 81
Mean's Land Nguta In Laughters 82
Historical Upheavals 83
Biological Barriers 84
Kitchens Of The Ketch Ups 85
Scenic Maps Parts 86
Signing My Death Lion And Hell 87
Alternative Triumphs 90
Edit No Story 91
Surgical Moils 92
1788 To The Gates Of 2028s 93
Federation Still Lied 94
Impounded Blacklists 95
Oral This Transcripts 96
Envy Puddles 97
No Classes 98

Anonymous Are Out Numbered 99
Travel A Fly Of No Return 100
Current Life Dress Maker 101
Caused Us To Be Collaborator 102
Saints Are Homeless 105
Deceived The Author 107
Times Off Hard Lovers 108
Resembled Loyalty's 109
Repetition Solitary Dad Where's Mum 110
Borri Is Fire Waru Is Fire 111
Mercy A Memory 115
Before They Said Hits 116
Concentric Blacks Fleets 117
Anthology Our International 118
Non-Pain In Rain 119
"Planning With My Flight..." 120
Vote No? Ho 122

Notes 125

MURGON BRAWL CHERBOURG BRAWLS

They out there, not hidden
Have you heard of that brawl?
Up at Murgon town
Have you seen the 20 15 or so?
Darkies cause a fuss and fight?
Well, they came and told
Me before I read a paper.
Some sisters bashed up a
Female cop hey.
Some cops dragged picked on
The wrong black man,
So they deserved what Bompi
They got hey.
Now there's this Jackie Joe
Saying them blacks who
Can't hold their grog bang
Brought the brawling on
And guessed what him say to media.
I'm a bit ashamed to be Aboriginal
For they should not have charged at football
Show games places
Well who started it
Cops speaks drunks started
Hit Hit Hit
Black Joe Jackie says all dri=unks
Started Hit Hit Hit
But Jesus was a drunk
Have you all heard, blacks
Drunken having a good time
Blacks, playing win or

Lose, sometimes can't
Hit, when called boong nigger,
They react fast
Have you heard of stirring?
Cheeky police office
Who wait for those loud?
Talkative blackfellas under the weather
Then bang into the paddy
Wagon or slammed
The police don't maintain good
Relations when you heard of
Bompi Bompi with Murris
Maybe all bad cops and bad blacks
Should go over goori for fighting ground next.

(To Kurt & Nanny Fisher, Sunday 8.39pm 2011-01-09)

"DARAN" "DARAN" FORBIDDEN

See, in golden nightmares the eternal
Shades are the same.
See in the vast moon eclipsing night, our day conveyed
Begin to climb the swift brief
Year to homes.
Be a fashion of arts
And be withdrawn in renewing.
The fingers of your hands are but
A birth to man.
Make hold of it and your life and he as your light.
But young love comes along once
When time allows a world in love.
Sure the darking sight of my eyes
Are to be seen only by what you read.
Now be of your own golden foresight because you are too
Loving towards a road.
Even if we see a land on fire
It doesn't mean the rain will fall.
The world is of more life than
Ever and tears are falling over their faces.
The boys are to be men when the day they love one
And all who live for joyfulness.
The girls are to be women
On the time of natural blood flows.
Through the lands we are to grade a "DARAN DARAN'"
Of animals' erotology living.
The dreams in times
Brings birds in fly this nests inner
The core of birth.

We all draw a photo of ever being beyond and above.
The shades of earth's
Plants are our sex in bodies.
You sit on a cloud and think a man will feed you.
You speak to a silence word to no one who hears you.
And we all feel a vibe inward around the sun and think that
Inside it people exist, live and breathe.
See now the man in the golden nightmares.
He has no life to his rights as a being.
But for one thing,
We all relive in a space of just passing over the worlds

(Sunday 9.30pm 2011-01-09)

CONSERVATIVES SELLS

Here is the Modern humorous
Aboriginal best known to be conservatives
And black students who just care bout getting
Their degrees.
Translate this and we get them thinking white
Not all are serious for their people's voices.
We will be critical of you live in white communities just for comfort
Conservative blacks will turn
To us for themes
But the method will be white instructions.
Sure them darkies have beautiful
Gentle faces of intelligence
But we both Ancient and new will out do.
Our excellence with sober
Wisdoms will brake
Arrogant illustrates
Now you conservative blacks
Think it's time for new ways
Where sunlight creates appeal
Where efforts be no more
Where opinions is a choose
And rich is sensibly reasons
Have live-in in luxuries.
So your Antithesis treatments
Comes clearly of nonsense
Writing we read by youse.
Part forgive rest in the divine
Trueness of our blackness
Yet conservative blacks are

Trying to be naive fighters.
Thinking they do in goodness for us
Seeing it as development for us
Here we are Modern blacks too
Yet we have these conservatism in
Some blacks in power decisions who
Just play white games.
We must denounce destroy these suckers?
We Aboriginal have folklore
And you tell us dat J.C. came over here,
This is not via Christianity.
Mythological we are
Native legends we are
The eccentric by white
Fairy tales is typical
But we are typical blacks
A mysterious adventurous
Human go sets white man
Came unincorporated in narratives.
Now here in 2019 their government
Wants to buy our land up
Northern Q.L.D. BACK FOR US.
Gee-shit aren't this tribally our
Rightfully own land anyway
People today misinform what imparts with maternalistic
Whites or yellows Japs.
Certainly this thing happening
To our land cultural moving flightiness,
Is a white classic?
Most think Aboriginal themes
Causes or declines and banishment is not neglected
Disregarded anymore.

As changed for the betterments
Of our blacks here and there
This the fake foolish of
Your 2019 societies.
They'll give back a skull or
Bones, but in long run
Take the mind soul maybe.
Most whites and some blacks are
Profoundly pessimistic viewing

(Sunday 10.30pm 2011-01-09)

BAM GAYANDI

Jealous greed's in lot a blacks' houses
Jelly sets in a cold black people hearts
Bitter wind blew malign land iced families
Bitten magnetic needles jetsam's naked natives
    Country of mystery tempest
From my eye from my dilli
Problematic oozes Blount wasted fight
    Teenagers' teens' tiny sir + miss
They're ah thousand coastal wilderness.
Destiny in dark JARJUMS floats
High in bush ethos dream in
Things of stone and coppice fields are
    Trundling rhythms vibes gammon love
Thing in melodrama Anglo-Celtic
    Sink in a dishearten nostalgia
Thinking negative Murri sound a word
    Are not continues
        Cos no love in a go dam school
Moon
Hillsides new time new age
Moon till hard blackfellas remote those
    Fretful nullity fainting
So we gush ambivalence gave by spirit=
Ngundarui tranquility balances pleasure
Thundered us dat blacks metamorphose
The white man society won't ever mould
Me writing or saying
I am non-tribal
For Irish name or whatever

    I gritty their world in look
Jealous I feel I'm over yet it's combative stir
The crow's dat banished whiteness mummies
    A Koori people bird gave me a
Human speech in mainstream near the Cree
The senselessness a woman dog gave was five flower
Of rarefied poison powers.
The dwindled lanes cuts your foot
    Small creatures exemplify earth love
Bitter air around those dat dares blacks
Bitter sound in hometown blacks rose
A invitation wham jam story
Countries slaved pressure perfect healer
Beast of mystic "souls came into mystic being down under"
A mystic bliss came over
A miseries darkness overspread reciprocal voyaged Bam

(Sunday 10.59pm 2011-01-09)

"HERE COMES THE TRANQUILITY INCARNATION..."

Here comes the tranquility incarnation
Vessels beyond entrenched oneness
You have verged and probe our
Horribly prostituted blacks of the 2021
Vanquished burdens are at your curious birth.
When I as a merited sensation vulture the
Inner craving of gracefulness
You will give me pleasant body
You will give me devotion
And I will have supreme lusting
Desire over your voyaged body
Inspiring private doctrines come
Perfection up submerged individuality
This flinging addiction of power rushes
To a lovelier spiritual plot.
My teasing supernatural vision
Of me will visit all humans
Woman's vessels entrenched oneness
Mystic mortality are resolving
At senses who farther into
The bottomless wild blackish
Pink dust sweet agonized sobriety
Now a smoke fumes you
Coming from a burning rose
The sperm of dat man is
Flush in pale creature whose underneath molten motions as germs
My naked explicit sex paused
At the lit golden body in

Morning bosoms.
I have conspired your twice weathered
Depraved body once before.
Now intoxicated by old educated superiors completeness
Your eruptions curves a ensiled
Satisfaction of your own reflection.
Now aroused in a sensible mentality
Your affection is stimulated upon
My physical racial body.
The art of my loving can't wander romantic
Curiously over to your vessels.

(Moon 7.00pm, 2011-01-09)

RELATED-OBEYING-ABORIGINES

Direction will come with blackfella action
"Dying ills some living"
Trial by relatives foresee our patience's
Tales by dem personally speaks
Rails of commitment is shown by
    Murri trust in lifestyle
Noongar brothers our lifestyle
    Is rededicated-dedicating struggle
We never beg no more peaceful dreaming
Ceremonies blacks more are memories
Murri business silently thinking sounds
    Are dead leaf a falling   happy leafs breeze
Those crushing past whisper in
    Will strike shuddered response
Those caused felt hurt
    I will curse until no hurt
Middle fear chills warmth spirits
Most high exhausted powerless
We build available stronger swish
    Old man old woman love-in actions
They younger lover over knowing
    Are hard-headed
Hey listened land awaits our created
    Choice and sense
The way is dark from there we tell you
    Courage now rages over pains
Directions will come with 'Abos' action
    Action in good acts come within black direction
Our union is the highest now

Our renewing is the highest now
"Die in ills some liven"
Mutual companionship forward steady
The way out of dim dark ugliness
Is devotional struggle even fight in?
For our earth our land our peoples

(Moon 8.00pm, 2011-01-09)

PARTNER TO WHAT TERMS

Land is the housing
Housing is the land
Conditions are continued
Stronger licences fresh in posies
Stronger legislative as if legs ant's shoved
Stronger breaches for badly profit
Township request clear commitment
Pro-independent parliament gave
Disadvantage determination
Process as views consulting works
As win and loose build yet ensured
Emergency transitional social elements
Is this response?
Gaps of consequential investment
Mutual, darkness in rainbow.
Bills come and vulnerable long-term
Livelihoods repeal even appeals.
Redeeming tabled impressments' widespread
Reason reborn assessor decisional.
Land in the hands, land in the hearts.
Penalties in pains to who's ashamed.
Signage laws approve respectfully
Those plan publish complement.
Treatment special harm or related been focus local and national.
Solution causing target diseases are proposed in efforts extensive
To the government's "enough is enough".
Reiterative feelings source are income
Man made trade + paper levels.
Regulation barriers administrative councils irrespective

Still leases the money + private camp holders,
As if tenancy were around for thousand
Household property pre negotiate
Our men fought for narrative country
Free from terrorist in own back yard.
Let us all see time's eyes non-war
Writer black red yellow sentinel.
Development the trainers of our soldier elaborated divinity in
High knowing, the battle as just howl louder to those if any
    indifferent.
Coalition to putting the casualties
In attack of the aggressor.
The dinner with red dogs was not like the red god's, citizens being
    acknowledge as statutes prized and expelled by pride.
Weapons in conquest feel no racisms.
The policy opportunity exiled the poisoned small pox minds
Reimburse Australia's seekers to commemoration on every banner,
Cavalcade modern admirers to be remonstrance.
Devotion prelude next world word as the revolution babe the
    egalitarianism
Blood presence fealty traumatised.
Our past men wars were to win freedom were free thoughts as,
Was long before time played
Winds off untimely lands.
Teach us the life where lights have no
Closured after wars life's

(2012-04-23)

⚡ LUCKY COUNTRY SAD LOOSE SOCIETY

Australia not own by anyone?
Australia not given by godparents
Australia not the future mooring morning=lovers
    when you'll war on poor's.
Australia can be better to the beggar in rich classes
Australia where's the carbon date tax refund off 100 thousands
    years with out rents' arrears.
Australia take the land away from dark people, the story still
    evade, our heart
mind kick the spirits higher.
Australia your sport man sport woman must be in your
    number out in the antilog Aboriginal's day walk run fly to
    cellmates first Australia first spirit of health first foot arm
    bodies to do it an do it right.
Australia don't be a yellow cake pussy's
Australia is a community not societies.
Australia not your country the countries belong all Natives
    yes it's your society stay there………..

(2012-05-22)

MAPS GODS TO WHOSE

City of life, rich is poorer of life
City of life Earth poor scroll return again
  World societies livers are orders too
    Loot cook bad lifeless births.
      City off earth smile every non owned
Dwellers, fat maps fat men fat gods
Food eaten at the poor no countries
  Nation as oneness
Where is the sun seen by mankind
  Eyes as birds fly the ground
To above the sweet noise city's
City off life rebirth the all in all
Equals cash in no face,
But bodies being all in all.
City where life says fast slow walks run every
Health at prices high low
City sound every mucus heat the
  Beat in thousand fire burn towns
(Bikies busy wounded by fates)
Food the music city off can dance.
Away with pain as planes cars bus trains
Skies awaken to no spirit book sell
Songs sang the city to life.
Peoples of no race foreseen human being one's
Love as no laws
City fought not life people,
Yet oppress without dictators ships

(Bangkok, 2012-11-08)

COUNTRY'S SUB'S NO SUSS TOWNS

   Mission bleeds we are.
Face book never touched my people face
      For done have these society's genets.
In this story people harmony without the man,
   Teasing till pressure piece ancient messages.
The very sound grovelling weary Australians.

No dead earth land seem relived
Dead worlds seem the death bet bed of all.
Brisbane blacks are sussing on star under feets.
Sydney blacks are blanch on suss under fools.
Melbourne blacks are no street name houses
Aid Alay blacks are suss in 49 gang stealing a sin
Darwin blacks suss light burned in letter rudeness
Perth blacks are suss never know first perished
Cairns blacks are suss no care or less to test the rich
Broome blacks are sussing pushing sweeping floods not danced.
Hobart blacks are suss when tree are unit the land of sea.
   No new year, every year the same
   Vote out; vote in today's 250 years boat people still cold old in hole
   Hot ten by me woods not burned.
Face book eyes where are art enter wine
Warmed only by killer mates sleep for the high solicits cell
     compared to the itinerant our grant money ran out.
Felled is the feeling when they are so blind the story was not touched.
Cause thrown fire pie in eyes is the cases.
Court's sub's no suss in towns I am the mission black that says
   this big O.K.

(Merton VIC, 1.00pm, 2012-12-24)

1967 ENCOURAGED THE RIGHT VOTE NOW?

Referendum who will vote for see —
Citizen to who will write the truth.
Refer what census over prohibition of us,
Who custom attitudes still stands by the old
White supply user vices settled life pig's style.
Policy don't work when first human beings
Are known to common all wealth.
Amendment whose act months of imprisonments,
Exemption what definition when eliminate was them official
Trying to get rid of my peoples, no matter what the indigenous
    adopt?
Certificates our restriction on evil by the white laws.
Powers in aspect are control protectors still 2030 to 2040
Give us our right is not the established times,
It's caste of wine beer boards widened the gabs and step fallen
    to gives us
No swinging pools for change in wear was the foot on our chins.
What public don't see our children's in life now is mad or insane
Even to vote on the big notes
Attain status be from they came as give all Australians the free day
Just be for the white man a child of his womans set a foot in
    our beds;
Have the vacation day now or never forever's hey.
Referendum the who will vote for this day and nights
Citizen what won't be silly to the truth to all in all

(Merton VIC, 2012-12-06)

"THE FAT FUNNY DUCKING TOOK MY WOMAN… "

The fat funny ducking took my woman and made her fat again
Made her sweat holding men as two times.
The fat belly spirits forget the slinky man who made her a garden
Now she lips other men sweeten their wife's lone nests
As the man sat pissy up the past even remembering drink tales
As if thing were ok after sex drunk alright keep under cover in her house
Fuck yelling in silence making him wild out over love to lust over duck dusk.
Her befriend was a need to know basis where beds are brighten by fear off her past seeing rocks foot held down under water giving more than needed.
Invasion by her she let by, for she said love the bad one that done worried her.
Well phone call what any more don't want to speak no more in other times
Well will she tell the truth where sex is at or where nature lasts for long times
Now she as other men women's on mind as if work time can not call to whole's call she await every morning every afternoon, night time but a lying tales.
No real text no real want to lie in bed any way.
No demerit puss for a lover's disqualification
I calculated a blind date been seen to by you big puss conviction
I offence the lust we had now enclosed body's shown brochure in the futures
Financial my loss can't pay back up employment or your lifestyle to be safe to obey lover's traffic social points.

Important details are qualification when peace unity is the lover's war over wars
What conditions.
She just blames the fat ugly drivers relevant depending in total vary periods accumulated schemes
On good behaviour for whose aggregate may be extinguished in result to the holdings
In supervising accept up an down look will she tell her man friends occur or disqualified electing whilst licence serve appropriate in lieu of sexy provisional applied hey fat girl where's probationary.
Now incurred effect twice surrender brought obtaining caring
The fat funny out back woman thinks she as the world in her fat bum fat belly fat lip fat boy friends after weekend years to a day, the particulars to who she wants not me to be her needs happy with them not me. ......Demerit lovers I'll pay

(Merton VIC, Thursday, 13-01-24)

AMPLIFIER AIMS OF CIRCLE

Enticing as a educate civilised
Gave personal property concepts.
Landmass hearts received architectures
For those unfriendly renders.
But function combines religious
Giving failing communities.
Mystic no more the brinks of exquisite sad whirlwind.
Frozen rapture times, came slices where abyss mountains swallow
Music, only children's clouds can sing heart growth.
Unscrew occupation where politics
Sends money voices in control
Unscrew fester ripple hate
Liberty a entice prism shade
Liberty a entice reflection earth fathers of indigenous exist.
Love man identity butterflies by city encumbrance tenderness.
For the strains the radiate must built action over words foreclosed.
Dormant the same old pain mole,
And let go matter burrowed deep.
Enticing times of aims encircled.

(Flying to Melbourne, passing NSW, Sorry Day, 2013-01-26)

IMMEMORIAL CONSERVATIVE

Rioted by the rights, Do it blacks insights into compelling
    writing a painting.
Morning by the light a mist wings a right
Cause rioted ways over sad tear so ear drop eyes.
    Pervade those ethic sucked worlds.
Lack people's slack strength.
Limited curiosity promises differences
Hey counteraction angered suburbanites
Revolt abstract riots, buttered up by
    Remedy of retaliations.
Be confidentially over oddness in panic
Be seasonal not crank fraud for,
    Voting servant to the governments?
Created levelled outlined laws are,
    Vibration manifests fests by guests.
Prosper corroborative reputable distress
    While answers are appointed.
Riot those silent in mercy complaints
Their lives condition attractive for me
    And you, yet bleeding change must
Organizes impression in with drawing
Overall availability were unfold
Don't have fun fuck hit the douses
Risk the riots tonight for the real fights.
In remembrance of our crowd flushed
Out of this systems.
Recline the firm folk black lore.

    (with LACEY YOCK BROWN, Merton VIC, 7.30pm, 2013-02-19)

CUT AN PASTE

Sitting here a-witting time to be mine
I write more art where painting as word of stories
Being put into statement makes we
Occupy profile others webs on sites
Interpretive by the readers before a written
Dictionaries is loved or hated is
Incorrect of the writer's act.
Flying collaboration by feelings
When my words not engage seems
Question translatively untaxed.
Then to merge trivial distinction over
Our comparing historical adjusting
Looks like an Internet net of twitter
Verbal lost cheaper revelations.
Sitting under the tree, where once
House was sat my clouds
Was once my word turn to log over
The rainbow disruption
Incentive was the publishers just
To money on the cost of loving
Screen played words.
We right the write to market all
New devices, so contributing
Can be easy on the lines.
Now myriad off advantages are
Experience at guess who wrote; but
Not who said it on hear sayings.
The mathematical answer in email

My mines find EBooks
In times, not central to constrained

(VIC, 5.00pm, 2013-03-14)

A—Stands for have a day hey no layabouts
U—Stands for you untied the uncles
S—Stands for sir sect the dirt no shit
T—Stands for tea let flour and tease
R—Stands for rebirth the reality re=box
A—Stands for Amuses ointment a vibe a la
L—Stands for what a hell no loyal for Lionel
I—Stands for I an I needs no invasion
A—Stands for Aboriginal the only race around
    And Australians Romans pick a box words
À la dart hey the Aust; lied to truth
A—stands for hey no Apology improve
Emotional blood on the lip from a computer
As a reputation for swearing
Things are private ever more
Yet presence stuffs dark characters employers
To be purely berates.
Option from the future see's death to
The old fools who incline others to
Boggy their child-hoods.
This as no opportunity
This as no opining
Where contact in literary many
Metropolitan fails, the imagining aspiration.
So epicentres are not recognised
Advantage Australians affair stands

(VIC, 5.30pm, 2013-03-14)

SWIFT TERRORLESS

Pre tend my mobs bobs in dobs
   Pre lend my sending not rented
Be a shell where no hell sprinkle
   Be a small mate in late ate in hate
Advance stomach midden of sobbing
   Distance tepidities feelings
Advance strong newcomers adjudicate
   To pay batted money to Aboriginal's
Advance trip's tired from buildings
   And not bouncers on the check outer.
Mother market the fantasies Mister whose
   Majoring whispers are gratitude
Of a-loud multicultural wrongs.
Market mums over central flutter
Warmness so strobes the robed.
Market get those commands where
The poor can't afford, then we will find rekindled laws.
Confirm ambience corridors seclusion
Seeing the rural sexy retreating
Convert humpty superb screens.
Confirm irrigation shone tropical bodies
So the sound home–buyer's
Are relaxed in laced.
Stumble close now to the daughters
Of the black man's avoid cock.
Tumble and baptise the justice to juices.
Now laughter at the way I wrote

Pre piss on ribbons empty of anxiety
And curtain high the gossip amblings.

(Merton VIC, Monday 1.30pm, 2013-03-25)

FOREIGN ADMIRATION

Those was comparing supering pains the same
    Almost accountable the sums of face to facts
When mentality is differs,
Spiritual in spirits spit patter playthings.
Those one after gave performing rhythm
    On platforms as a cries to stop cries
As a word to stop categorized wars.
Are still comparing same oppression,
Look our race went through different
    History made up pervaded
Expressing, pains the same curs lovers.
So generative no change when conservative
    Are sucked calibres for frustrations?
So young people not born yet see
    History was a stone rock sand
Thrown in seas to be rivers
Even when the mountains
Are roads over the rainbow experience?
Those relating belief story of it
Oppression, think two years
Same as the insane that proves
All the bourgeois are humans.
Those Madame thanks-giving for
Recognition in classes not
Rebellion high mind bodies' agreement.
Those live in abundance will
Dance sing capsize regenerative
Our cause in more mistress.
Now charming comparing amazing

Silent gave determined echo
No God or Goddess is relative?

(Merton VIC, Tuesday 4.30.pm, 2013-03-25)

LITERARY EMBARRASSED

Man's origin became the dust epitome
   When void hankering intellectual dipped.
Man's origin blood joy mortal inglorious
   Flights stained divinity sciences
Now damnation diffused solar metrical
   Gave us observed grandeurs
Now tempest horrible recedes are
   Interpretation by question monologue
Man phantom monument concave
   A million radiant descriptions
We sublime dramatic illusion for
   Wonder full didactic intentions
Why enslave intelligence to be tenderness
   When the pursuer library old-established oriental lakes.
Why the products of adventurous
Complication is romances.
Man's reformist are pummelling the deceptive comical
   advertise compeer.
Man's atheist republican trance makes
Ordinary nonsensical satirical.
Where execrated languishing troubles?
Times in voice will revise and startle the non-readers.
Man's extraordinary argumentation will
Odium the ludicrous astonishment.
Man's mad condemned private public
Perfect are reviewer are insinuation
Where nail consequence are orchestrated
A big literary embarrassed.

(Merton VIC, 12.00 am 2013-3-27)

PERVERSE APPROAHES

(Do always) YABURUHMA what the (eagle) MIBAYN (earth)
    JAGUN JUGUL
Does in (early) GITTA GITTA (morning)
    YAWUN (just dark) makes
Romantic thematic is dirty energising
Interwoven by coheres of rich narrates.
Our MURU (nose) NALU NANDIR (nighttimes) smelled
Thousands futures life's air by the
(Milk) NAMAH DIMIN we drink.
GARMU more rivers, YILUM YILUM more mouths.
Roots wood and find the words
Before teased worlds inexperience,
Our sharing negotiatives.
Many are spectators on perversion demands
So accomplished readers attend those needs
In psychoanalytic bring lifes.
Sadism in enjoyments of pains are occupied
  By obscener gaze acts.
Restored political sources dead dance
Our people's borrowed strategies.
The discursive feelings zones are
Precarious to us when restoration
Is obliteration by rewriters?
(Flame) JALNAY (smooth) BARBAN our protest
    jalum bira (fish hooked)
Possibilities rare themselves as vision
Birth the new earths not hurt.
Deform all settlers' portrait attitudes
Refractive eyes dilli's binna ears are

Identities in sacrifices now.
Respect pleasure those privileges not ages

(Merton VIC, 10.30 Friday 2013-03-29, on the day J.C. got killed)

ENROL A PEN FRIENDS

There are lack songs
    Instruments cause pains
      Echoes are text in selling
        Laurel is cruel to poets
          Wealth heats poor heavens
            And dialogue poor waves
Advice picture agent out
  For line by lines
    When done as the final story.
There are marvellous writers
    When harvesting the unique meeting places.
Big talks are layout for small talks.
Mapping my our futures, are hard by the easy
    Get long with in the middle classes.
Performer feed feature for films unwritten.
Now the unwieldy words
    Are instruments for passion?

(Merton VIC, 3.30pm)

STOP THE SOAP MEMORIES
(LASHES EN-TONY TOIL)

"Shall the poet bite the fang so Liberal to be Liberty."
Liberal wise of spite
Might we be your future's night?
Run your hand finger over our arm in care,
Liberal already cynicism bit of lips that
Prattled the sages off mouths legislate.
"Paper noose the nose that pawn death to vote"
Liberal be the liberate decrees of papers
Firing squad chandeliers a light.
No death to liberty while Liberal is governmenting.
Liberal lick the last vote from the
Plods boat and bejewel crook as
Simpleton parliaments.
Lay side by tongue of pride
Where pity is no corral to speaks.
Liberal lexicon our free minds to
Bodies' dialecticians are jackal
So surprise is mountainside.
Liberal a tone for the craftsman will dream
The house first to courts.
Leeches common on laws Liberal really
We groin your coins.
Commandments are mead to brake
Come Liberal comedy of comprehends
Dovetail imperilling import our
People pocket to power power by the hours.
Liberal don't postponed the fight for custom
Are your dams in deluging rivers of sky-embalmed tomorrows?

Liberal dices the rice for all our rights.
Libs be real libs see now the lights soap our memoires in the lashes

(Merton VIC, Sunday 2013-04-07)

MINDS OVER POETS

In life of overs we have us,
Obersevation eye meet the ears were justice niches
    Our all in all bodies.
Interruption love's needs when war as feelings
Being pulsed by time bring the wined hearts
To describe UnumProvident rushing wind
Temperature in helpful needs.
In light a design cell in a million nerves
Us native bloodline asset recognised.
That the century of futures is tendency
To be an invited comparison.
The deepest mystery perform memories all
    In an integrated picture.
But chemical behaviour complicated
Software human mindfulness,
But to give connection in neatly summarised
Fluids make the suggesting scientists
Are possibly elsewhere.
The word in phenomena limit despite
Bring practise gain instigative existence.
Now a personality-manoeuvring peak
Of physical climbers absorbed spearhead
An evolution to dreaming.
Having normal transcend our remember
keep waves appearance to lead
The talent unusually brilliant.
Seeing an impossible dreams means
We are frequently of abnormalities.
Now after read this no white man wrote

Independent to these lips for the ears
Now after workout what I wrote, no self,
Natural divide complex creatures
Made a state of consciousness.
The laboratories in mechanisms remain
At every radically stated altered startling.
In life full to master's peace unity
Trance us to rare concentration.
Yet buying conceive by Mother Nature
We find painters talk sing and touch.
Yet no exceptional individual is without
A people.
So boredom in the centimetres sounds
Are still acts of artists in surgeons task
To cast clarity absolute colleagues.
The challenge to any combination will
Hill exceed condition, being myself
Brushes activity to many instinct.
The reward in high-risk certainty ride
The hide, so flow to low focus, becomes
   Electrically quiet.
Patching survival say the living is easy
For a greater amateur to match discovering.
In part preoccupation strange terms
Are for own sake to past over beyond.
Insight black matters molecules
And the source is lands not entertained
In dark minds sums are induced by
Mathematic ideas for judgement.
No distraction of pain will give your
Excited make-believe techniques to
Be the forever entirely distortion.

No ignore sense of euphoria became
An account of intuition, so common
Meditation must effort pure found ways.
I lifeless inspiration gives new blossoming
Willing engrossed compose.
The composition of this is paper over papers
Giving rudiment margin preferences.
The style is calligraphy artistic words
Avian the world as passageways.
Now fades the construction assiduously
Now flower bowers the attract adopt.
MANFIRE WOMANFIRE

(Merton VIC, Saturday 2013-04-06)

THIRTY YEARS FROM 1983 AND STILL GROWING A TREE ROOTS

She was not pretty but still pretty
Hair off red touching yellow lips
While her hidden black skin of her
Past ride the spiritual sexy looks
Her eyes gave, into two legs
Short long wide when needs
To open lush flashed fork
By sweet careful ears.
She faith a lay, by the staying
Featly on her feet,
No two-time man awaited her
Smiling luring,
She fables funny at figs feral
When loving was fabricated.
Now members fade little by wits
As her body remembers arms
Lifting away sad nest on
The bum sat down outside.
Up jump a fly butter by flying
Star fire into back bedrooms
Sleeping, to climb to on step
Bed dream awake favourite.
The wind below her finger speaks
The darling blemished flower.
As sacred shine rivers wedge her
Lips for that ever feeling she
Think now happy attitudes to distract.
Face by parties times looks, she sees

Mirror shuffled by fragile non-fears.
Face to years her feet blunt a prose
For the memoir of one man's times
Not used by her piecing.
Adopted by astounding courage in
Needs a free-fall complex
Profoundly font now to
Narrative frankly wholeness wisdom.
She arts reconnection brave ageless
Fading demons away by her
Derives to hold irretrievably the
Changed adult hood.
Knowing she can't live in past
To ability her essence to
Bust unique lyrical verse
Uphold.
Yet chants of scramble truth
Signals her voice to laughter joy
Yet chant dance linger the trails
She wanted to give this formality.
Exemplary the tongues once rehab
By sex to sex when good of
Company.
Her life guardian watcher never
She meet, Yo but survive as
Tap on windows silk message
Came the birds arrive the massage
Gave in circle extinct.
Relieved was now celebrated to
Taken on who will make the
First move on raw deserves
Fakir fairs flow remorse

She rode the horse over to
Silver expects, while the four-wheel drive back bush
Grabbed the pants in practise targets.
Freedom in 17 years, now in
Rain hail she priced possession,
I remember you sweated on
The mother of your childrens
Now kick me the distressed I
Never really wanted hey,
All those dead deaf eyes,
Now bruises for the beauty
On the shadow dresses,
Were drunken joints rolled?
For your care while she
Sunrise the food of hope looping
More forward to release
Faults cringe and cries.
Now the illuminated damaged
Goes by, with words painted lay
Art to art till churns turn
Feeble free nomadic fashion
Bash dictates gently red escapes
Avoided foetal file single
Survival heavens we enter
United by our lusting
Broken scratches and screaming.
Folding gypsy Fei can we lay faith
Faith in a bed gate constellation
In our secret dearest faintly
Rest calm soul eclipse sweet
Soft dull but glowing victorious.
Can we spin our breath delights?

All night by full fire hearts,
That's why fallen star have a
Orb on meeting enchanted murmuring
That's why intimates takes lots of
Lime time in paradise forever.
Well as a old man lulled in
Your could have been mind
But I have dreaming paints
When I sexed other womens.
They ask you think of roots off
A past girl had before.
No moon lying on earth
Gave no hurts,
No genuine eternity evidences
The once was once so short
No throned bush city contributors
Can give our hour on miniatures
We summered the cold notably.
Your manifold working must empires
The last years in the we
Must appropriate ok.
Symbol are imply, yet unbounded
Keep the faith gypsy Fei always laughing.
Will you let abstraction scatter away?
From any future vague in our quoted.
Will you let we elude mystic reality
And far float substantiate.
The desolation of loneness never comes
Now the exquisite tinted poems
Are of unchained conceptive.
Overture your composing multitude
Gypsy Fei in delicacy distinctions.

Overture passage a probably connects
So we can sense in tenderness
Request for friendly tributes.
The styles is you, forecast in stared
Duty in volume brought by our
Appearances if privileged.
Mimicking my body to your mouth
Down my ascended pinnacle,
I will passion degree in non suffered
I will costume your melody to
Venturous sexy colours of
Spread on the imputed binds.
Cannot wait to endurance your
Gracious motion in conjuring us.
Now I'm quivering the feathers for
Us to limb gleam white revels.
I the finals acts, take me down
And invest my festal Gypsy Fei flushing
Our cheeks so emblem in every forest.

(Typed by Jabreeni Fogarty on 2013-04-07)

METROPOLIS EXERTION

His burden was water wind mild by despair
While she wept to steal many monotony.
His commonly dilemma gave manner over
   Courageous mistress, just when fear got dejection.
Emerged by the pages a shadow of recover
Gave a languish delicate brief perfect
Intellectual colour of acquaintances.
She then tempestuously gentles savages
Many feelings into entertaining.
But by this biography society done
Was amused in the eccentricities.
A mazy metaphysical supplement
Entangle adoration so lustre that
Women run for the sympathy mans.
His satirist were gray hairs decayed
Yet in all paradoxes the ironical criticism
Was full of ghastly life's interpreted?
Now she recede unholy whirlwind by
   Her own spun pains.
Now repelling atmosphere of moths
Butterfly in bright mischief.
Water drank nothing when time lasted
For rich people strange changing.
Wind look for air, as quotation sang
Expresses for the enthusiasm boys.
Unveiled mild despair bring a pair of
Method to a medical controversy.
While she electromagnetic her lovers
Monotony sketch tongues, be bare ......

(Merton VIC, Sunday 6.00pm, 2013-04-07)

REGISTER DONATE

1. N.T. Important to now have language from enlist
   To our big speaking languages to and from.
2. Have days set aside for our heroes and womens
   Why not have national holiday for our writers
3. Fund on and on to cultural literature to bring
   Out book of stories and political always
4. To find unity to unite our different
5. Songs are sang so must be written
6. Give help to the histories to rewritten
   And correct other writers
7. Who write for us speak done sing for us
8. The constitutional intake our memorandum
9. Fee from non-Aboriginal writers
   Must be given to us, just like non-Aboriginal artists.
10. Know who we write for, after local, we go national.
    Be it cities or country towns were done are not there hey?
11. That society look, more to black writers
    By promoting a week national for our young.
12. Pub ushers fund a travel bus of writers to promote.
13. Have reading in every community towns
14. From N.T. writer must meet writers
    Every writer is not push button
    To be master of any words unity is
    Important speaking even painting has stories,
    Best told by the worker hey;
    The mind writes every day
    Same as the world goes around
    It's just to wise it and word it.
    Justice to most seems words

But paper man makes the action
The laws are all over shops
To keep life times are hard
When food games are higher.
To have a light, we must burn or set fire ago.
15 We as first Australian writer have all sound Australian
Written on the line behind us, to gather all the wronged
Written and practice to us on notes.
We can bring down the bad
16 Time for author to ride a bus to every town big and small to promote writing.
And let know how where about
17 To get best selling works every where
No matter who are the black writers?
18 The white other writers take time out for black fella writers
19 To cross any frontiers we must never turn out white or betray our stories for a payment.
20 All intimate memoirists as to have black fell outcomes.
Not two places past white sex or friends.
21 Most time past tense are hour ago cold feeling made wronged thoughts,
What motivated a voice to process?
When no rights are said or wrote
22 For us to get pushes can we go?
To our pushily black without getting knock backs.
23 Where is the money for endowment or to get people to help prepared?
Works in future what happens about whose is a poet writers

(Written in N.T. for the First Nations 2013-04-22)

WORKSHOPS NEEDS A NATION'S FIRST HEY

Family are sexual future if not policies
Family
Is not a race?
Brothers are not everything
Sisters are not everything
Mothers are earth arm legs foot
Was the blood runs hair down to ears?
Fathers are at times not men
At times their lover down and out
Cut the truth to the care
Family who are families sometime
Looks for nations.
To food friends in ships finds water
In tears leave baby's laying to be covered.
Funny wife seek life's
Funny husband seeks life
The children's writing free, dancing free
Singing free living thoughts free
Makes the family love on family.
Yet rules on up grown, bring most down,
But seeing those up higher
Gives a class where glasses are blind.
Hey families are running to be a families are
Running to be a families to those as no families.
Do we forgive those hurts of family who
Hurt people who unite families.

(Written at the Eye of the Storm Festival 2013-4-25 to 28)

OLIVE PINK FLY OVER SUMS

Was land when fenced?
Was love when flawed fenced
Was feeling when fears fenced
Where the houses when mouths are shut
Being told by ourselves seem made
The eyes see two ways over
Being holding the leaves fall by
The morning after night gave
Better insights.
Being near those of no stories
Suffer the minds wall to hall
As peoples of all races see
Together nesting a thought.
At no time found friends to be
Smells touch and slayings.
Love dress up for him and her
While filling lone one on one
Gave peace luck off the draws.
Fenced lay by lay changed
How we spend in shops down the roads.
Money on money fear made cries so crimes.
Wear out those inneundo in
Timing unity to unite
Sets Alice Springs

(Written at the Eye of the Storm Festival 2013-4-25 to 28)

VERSION OF THE PROGRAM

Short changes didn't make us compass
Unacknowledged memory was legislators
Globalised words in claimed
Challenges we barned injustices
Complex drives rewrite surface
No filmmakers can see verse
What the poetic license wanted
Was next century?
Sure really you did do that to
Our minds, that why our bodies
Are fighting, but not to kill each
Other, we might sleep alright
Tonight without payments.
We are stay in written laws
We are staying written as love.
Unacknowledged speak the tongues
I found prisoners are in society
So call free care cosy it became
Uncaring unloving the better is
Cost of whom tomorrow brings.
I found the best was not giving
The less any of the best.
This seems sad in gutter lifeless
Ground no matter what the towns.
Brotherly hard buys.
Sisterly hard buys.

(Merton VIC, 4.00pm Thursday, 2013-05-01)

TRAVEL AN ARRIVE

Bird has dreams
When done dreams as humans
Mornings as voices were done
Are woken for dead.
Nights rest up for the futures
Fight voting for higher words
In the woods green being burn.
Now birds voice is songs
For all the wronged times.
So to be as good unto those
Paying for free music and
Poetry without wages was
The keys to the cars' childrens.
Be the bird not caged
Be the being not been sized.
Sitting under sky where clouds
Is not seen blue hot heat?
Eyes sweating water, my feet
Hands wants to hit my face side to side
To ask will there be earth friends or
World of lost souls …
Birds have screams in silent
Of the human talkings.
When all thoughts are not the dreamers
Taken by the mind the lone body free.
She goes from here not writers
He goes from here not painters
Bit there people go off singing
But there people go off dancing

She goes from here reading
He goes from here seeing
Pictures being a movement

(Merton VIC, 4.30pm Thursday, 2013-05-01)

FIRST NATIONS AUSTRALIA WRITERS WORKSHOP

Notes Musings and Inspirations
Space on notes the tone is loaded
As power go by the flowers
Are dead to the face and sand creative
Yet the body lives dirt
Yes the aliening seeks sweet between
As lusting dreams not yours
   Is a trespass stories walk the looks?
Were rainbow kisses lips?
Make the poor the word doors to be the laws
And rich of hearts wealth to be a breeze,
Wisdoms hair is curly and teased
As power sea and land arms eyes
   Down on feets for peace,
Sad face smiles for one go
Shine a thousand laughter
Because on the bone space where lands
   Are mined by timeless hugging.
On my bodies I have one body to make my man.
Has power high and low want
The grass below to evergreen.
Lets unity feed our every space to the children's race.
Now mouth holds back the drawing
   Off song in all in all times,
Lone bones are apart of writers
White Black Brown Red Yellow forever
The Women kind to mankind.

(Of the writers' inspirations, Brisbane 2013-05-09)

CONNOISSEUR

They are excursionist on our culture
We are in a degree of velocity
You recoil in a ricochet of
Love to retroactive beliefs
Was satellite progressive?
Tractions stop you'll
Find our gravity
Being convergence to your
Admissions is what influxes
Our distillations.
The discharge baths in bright
Prostrated bloodiness
And our depressions are
Shortcoming in transmission
And our rotation turns to a
Plunging dizzy cyclone
We are spirits in levity
This globe wide by massive
Textures are becoming a
Friction with nature
At the delta we die
At the peninsula we live
Your vaporisation of lives
Won't corroborate within us
They dogmatise the blackfella
And upshot miscalculations
Even presumptions are made
In a scepticism way
Our communications is to our Murris

Our doctrine is ours to Murris
Our faith or professions is to Murris
But your doubt is yet a white
Man's discredit
But you assent knowledge
Of philosophy theory and encyclopaedia
For higher blackfellas to proficiency
Well these intellectual faculties
Are unsophisticated to our Murri
Imagined realistic minds
They are substantiated precision over
Our veritable culture Murri
Just exactitude illiterate maniac scholars.

(Merton VIC, Sunday, 2013-05-12)

"CAPITAL IMAGINATIVE"

Enter a world where lavish quest
Are made.
Enter the word first to wilderness
As lovers are discovering modern experiences.
Edged by always redefining the face of luxury,
But humbugged at humble branding people.
In exquisite histories we sense
Instance of the poor industry being
A tradition for money can buy.
In any artisanal common links
We screen many sirens as
Association to adventurers.
Quests are essence to know where
One on all gives innovation.
Cutting a commissioned to the bone
Embraced were the bodies.
The fashion here must let heritage be breathable.
Now over timely impervious quotes
You'll be that typical fantastical
Maker to dress a create.
Credited the label as bells trade our technology,
Where's the lavish coat of born essentials?

(Saturday 12:00am, 2013-05-18)

VARUNA HOUSE

Mountain came to the blue feets
Mountain came to the blue eyes,
Eleanor was not a dark woman
Eleanor I seen in dream thrown
Papers to Aborigines, as if lollies
Were given written Mountain are shifts.
Her timeless mouth as not been
Heard or seen by the great K Walkers
Of our writers, arts were lift were no tear.
Yet the sense of justice seem
Who was the last Murri writer to sit at her house?
Hell doors rang the pen to befriend a future's time.
But for what feeling or thought when so short of staying.
To suffer make no lit lures.
Eleanor full natives were every where in these lands.
The peace in written forms
The bush birds sky so dark on raining cold hot even
Lonely days, injustices suffers not the just.
As readers lay in text to sounds not written,
No book No cooks.
Eleanor I can't see your ways had past gully trees or valley.
At the houseplants feel death as placed life to birthing anew?
She was madam dark but wrote for social dark man's rights
Whose will bevies theses writers?
From hills to lip off mountain mouth
Came the first Australia writers Eleanor.
From your yellow mellow ghostly home.
I wanted to read out aloud my words of fight.
Cause the yardman worked for you Eleanor was a dark man.

So asking was he taught to write or just wages as we done
 that to write hit down for histories to know we had one or
 two around.
The leave are fallen to the tune off summer may make all
 write as arts are dying to not be photo any more by dark
 overseas looks alike.
A lean on the income writers in presents is hard when money
 can't pushiest my poems to you Eleanor.
The year 1901 moved me to go away from the city in 1985
 just to stay alive.
I thought your home was in bush but found it's as newborns
 everywhere.
And apart of the town made paper + wind chimes.
Seen so camped as ant as the kittens was scoring the children
 of another writer.
Blue colours are under my feet the eyes are dark with door by
 caves man made, to have steps a platforms already used.
The laughter was hard to hear animal's bird but the rushing
 howling winds air in my body to give another body song
 sang written words to the woods dead,
Yet ear closed to a cries of wording unrewarding restless which
 south happy shriek lips haired by not shaved takings.
Now I leave Eleanor not my in-laws
Now I let my spirit not pen in the books of your wanting one
 to typo the ways whiteflies write.
Thank Eleanor for the maid lay but,
Hum I Murri man a writer's ways.

(Eleanor House Varuna, Katoomba, Monday 11:30am, 2013-05-20)

SORT OF SORRY

Sort of sorry tears on drops
Were no eyes?
Sore cries
Walk pass the changed season
Sing passion to the changed leavening.
Mouths lay at the below eyes of beds.
Now writing is unwritten
So ear in took raw deals.
Then as a stood sorry people
Said no more tears.
Smiles embraced the truth for saddest
Wiped an extinct body.
No sorry business changes things
No loaded crying stops crimes
Walk pass the changing seasons
Walls seek space for the lonely faces
She saw pain in a lane of flyaway planes.
He sewed rains drops fallen by
The baby's unborn restrings.

(Sydney N.S.W., 6.00 am, 2013-05-26)

DISTRESS FRAYING

Fabulous whistles came in conversation
Defeating boring journalist was the ones who won awards.
Fetish document were ones who tug voids of false promise.
They came surveillance the way we wrote.
As blacks fell as anonymity gave subliminal execution violent.
Now their reader's truism was air crafted for corporate poets'
    high rises.
But refugee haunts the castes in concrete compel jungles.
But retreating hidden ties must come out to bloodstream in
    compete narrative.
No entering a stronghold attacks.
But the dollars can buy desertion Oh displacement in forgiving
Gifts written for futures engorged.
Will the incoherent polyvalent our kind in fabulous lifes?

(Flying to Melbourne from N.S.W., 26 May 2013-05-26)

THE COUNTRY ANYWHERE RACE ON RACES

Racist are not childrens
Racist are not Mothers
Racist are not Fathers
Give unity peace a chance
Racism is a sick disease
As a place for Non humanity
Racism as no race in Australians
For the first race is the only race.
Racist are instil by cheaper cap chaps
And those that joke on slip mouth are drops of sin bad food
    bad bodies of all ages.
Racism owned up changes the pace off no space
As the ship code to learn.
The ray of the sun shines for all under on solar.
The earth equally birth human
Yet the world's laws class those poor minds backwards,
When a racist sit with a first Australians proud
Of one race made a lace to lust we all comes from womens

(Merton VIC, morning, 2013-05-29)

ADVANCE THOSE ASIAN AND PACIFIC WRITERS POETS

As a Murri writer pitch fee in carvings
Asian unity we need is most important
They are the beings on top of us an on the side of us.
At our arms is the Pacific of knowing
We need to unite for rights in all writing powers.
Our Asians are on our earth if we walk under the seabeds we
    sleep together
Think where there's no sea the waves of our humanity is the same.
Most of this Asian Pacific is in fights just like loves that was taken
    from them.
Most times the spirit of unity is not walled or housed but air free
    smell free and giving a shared stories.
Life at all times shown must have no different, but there are the
    bright lights, when we are blind.
Asian is not cassation
Pacific are not anglosacktion
The peace of mind was a balance in space respect the times of the
    once timeless minds.
Can the truth of Asian Pacific writer give us justices of causes?
Yo if they don't get out work in their communities then the
    punishing world is at a lost.
So black fell writers this sacred future timing is important.
Remember in school we were taught they whites run them.
Will not true, wave have tunes
Our dancing not same, yes but thing can say and feel.
Our looks are not same but we see in painting art looks don't
    mean we apart.
Just see them real reading our stories our culture of what a fight

makes to be right.
Asian we can love on open eyes
Pacific we can love on open arms
They weren't our oppression
We know here lot bugged like the white man's peoples.
But that not the ones on homeland
Our skies in outback here beds and houses their skies.
The rain of road ships trucks all the days off all foods.
Delightment nights in fashion of opposite
Many souls' wants are to be unhurt unsafe offences of the desire to
   unity of the heart to art writing our Asian mobs have done in reply.
Our bodies spill the tempers but the spirit is one.
The moody Pacific mingling in our
Countries are negative at times
Yet these shinning sail them away says are sometimes can't stand
   their own peoples.
All people of Pacific Asian are star travelling poetry, but the
   destination get contemplation.
All Pacific Asian needs our first Australia words to fill their emptiness.
A thousand pages in the food dish will feed the mind body as one.
Require our bush land sea sky without a cost to cut your bloods.
Reason now Asian Pacific letters to us natives down under not of
   sorry uncountable.
Capture our song mouth lip in our written sweat drop off the spear
   pen we given.
Let Asian knowledge refinement to our first Australia writers.
Make our books be the beach to lay on.
Make the millions turn the pages our Pacific Brother Sisters writers
   learn and action to us, Asian as not drafting a trees felling over
   pain sad and down and outers.
Scream to the injustices quieted by birds in flying over the
   perpetually aggravation.

Don't like the lit bug Aussies,
Hum began to like the Asian Pacific forgive but don't forget.
Don't like the collar reserve sir to the loudly thunder statures.
Pacific some trash our calendar histories,
Yet most of them know savagery is a wall-to-wall things.
And the sea makes all inland the body of men and women.
Asian history must be on our side for future frail fake are not civilianise.
The words here is to rib the rid of bone requiem deceit in the rackets.
Asians are not my or my people's root yet flowers grow eye for an eyes.
Pacific are not my feet to eat, yet praise be it, to the writers not white in minds + bodies.
Coming back to poems over seas, yes the Asian Pacific touches our fingers without we know.
Half the write it's not gods or goddess just same as land love, when a rainbow is felt by the two people's the down under people walk and talk sing and dance the dust on the pages of histories futures.
We cut the trails off for the smell to be tongued all around the Asian Pacific worlds.
They were never boat people but cues to cuss and shared to share.
The Makassar came then stayed so we live equal passion and ate blood on blood drank the earth as writers to today.
Some kill we had in need not for power over powers that be.
Bourgeois Asian sits a write poor at the doors life's still die
Bourgeois Pacific sits on grass head thinking their freedom is the tongues they speak, well-written word must unite our respect too.
Mocked as nothing off shores, we last strong winged sails from shores to shores epics anew to write.
The warm beat on ward unawakened the sense in clearer washed skies.
Asian Pacific stories of the homesick
Aspire the creation unstained.

Asian Pacific attains our noon moon's recoiling colour crews to be lacerated by our mythologies.
Banished now those ambush settlements away from a chained writer's fears.
Bewail our progression painted to sing dance the one possess in peace over wars of grief.
Bound and adore our call for our poets to condemn flack fades of history awaking.
Monument the trust of patient and see our races unbridled.
Reappeared the repeated memories where no games are drop to knee.
The Asian Pacific volunteer are paid by the society vaporises.
We crawl not the injustices to arm our fingers and hand on legs for we yearn face on face rhyme to fierce any dodges of our writers.
Long lives the history of the struggle funny or wild to attack conditions.
Asian Pacific you all are the originality
Enfold the valleys in lust and rages
The country on earth is all that gives generation the chance to write and arts.
Shape our unity with perfect visionary give maturity to the immaturity other writers are old in the wall of racisms.
Mountain the unseen Mountains in our writers' poet to rich on every Aborigine wish.
From the dawn of futures to the Australia dedicated longings,
We still must affectionate our Pacific Asian writers' quarrel darkest mining to suddenly give hope over fury kept.
Fortune are moved by famous gallantry to stop genocides,
We must dominate all authority
Never surrender prophetic to the reflection of oppression
We must courage our welcomed one on number so high.
Customs are to carry on more so than the drunken stupor older chiefs.
Now speak of the harmony Asian Pacific's

Bungalow all poor and unrest the brigade,
Harvest the learners even grabs soil in all barefoot victorious to rejoice rein in return.
Blunders those evil when the writers are burial; in shroud to justices by poets not massacred.
False peoples say they are ministers not the truth of peoples on peoples,
So stirred the ancestral emotions.
Let the Asian Pacific warriors live message UN broken.
Let the Asian Pacific warrior's faith the barely crawled belly of mischievous.
Come Brothers of the Asian Pacific writers pleasant our pride for a truce in a thousand devour years, no colony can con.
The tall tales are Europeanism to blame for steering hopeless taste and treaty's surprises.
Dreamtime multiple declare all mistakes be a past tears for those unfriendly warpaths.
Familiar our write-to-write together now Pacifica Asian's narrow and bigger……….

(Merton VIC, 2013-6)

JOURNAL VERSION

Nuka children not just the futures
Men and women old of age are too,
Well is what I just wrote.
On this day I want get we wild
Where no name are said
On this night I want we not whites
Where no passion heard
On this future I want we to live
Was positive rain to dry beds?
People are not painting are still
Rating us to art
Where bodies work words on the word
Some can't write, lot can't find words.
The readers swim to win.
Most pay rent and at the end
Small food small life long planning. (Fat pans fried)
On the song lines are latter
Now not tuned by the now.
Living lifes for another make no right.
Lost voices are look readers
Lost voices are lawless under
Right wing tones, left wing fly.
On this power play, came a fighter's meal, no sit to sit.
On our all love's day
Came happy smile without
Drug or smoking
One day lip one night the future bright.

(Merton VIC, 10.30am Sunday, 2013-07-01)

ENCOUNTERS CONFLICTS

Copyright don't makes the typing
Getting works means write first
Up of the work, gives copyright.
Interventions are vents for not me.
The brain to work belong to
The hand pump blood from the tipping toes,
To sew means rows.
If think own for creative
Words over war thoughts
Peace using unity for the reading future
To work on the right way to feeling write and arts.
Copyright is not a cop
Right wing fight fly up to skies to drop the goods.
I have never copy white,
Writing or art to give touch feel or loves.
Just here to kill their pain laws awaken the blames.
Cannot reconciliation with a politic which has no loves,
Or out come jobs.
Oh well jobs are copyright by rich outcomes anyways.

(Merton VIC, 12.30am Sunday, 2013-07-02)

GALLERY MANSIONS MURDERS

While they have festivals
We are dead with a cent of life's happy nestings
Some of them are cast of cost of death
While alive trying to jingle the guilder.
Age old even young devises in racism
Are going to be roped by hanging at the sparkle
Of truth as a roots.
While the blood stain seat by the taxi
Friend believe in fielding fascism
For the cost of the drive.
Racial believes are and ants racists
If taken learned to be not a histories.
Mean while festivals obliged by trade racism
For a differ is but a cop out, deny deny.
Retrieved misery hates mate no relate for even a disease mens.
The wounded skin on any knife brings healed waste.
In times of horror no breathe as rights
While festivals breezes beauty to the afternoon chills,
We warmth a despair moments for those who fought months ahead,
Over dew to sunshine rehabilitation.
Productive process cages forgotten life's festivals.
The guardian fate of racist is late
To festivals please explain

(Merton VIC, 3.30am Sunday, 2013-07-02)

A GLANCE

Lay my days away
Yaburuhma women's of my past
The grunting mission present futures man
Says tongues are tighten by the home spun political
Nods of a hovel give in to them, who taken your lands and personally.
The ego of eggs stubborn in breed
Was changing for higher educating.
Now big business wants us to fluent
Our decades to come, with job on job to have blown a canon
 of literary.
Give annotated struggle, so brilliantly our new collection of young
 can respect
Lifetime work as get it done now.
Important poetry is proper when poors are significant in praise.
Give recognized voices of us by our flighted publicities
The grunted mothers wants are needed
Those grunted Father wants are needed
Melt no plans when matrix
The writer is a lyricism.
Say what on my tongue, be from we
Done or said it, lay my days away grunted

(Merton VIC, 6.00am Sunday, 2013-07-01)

CONDENSATION A PIERCINGS

We are opposite to simpler living room
Catastrophes pouring problems over
The insurance we differ by causes.
We will never conceited to anger
Or mortal wrongs to love.
Complacency she gave as convenient
Well nuts and bolts are charade.
I value the prisoners' poems when
Free stories to freedom our all people to
Never be jailed.
General illusion of words names
Play blind on eyes and mouths.
No multitude in distressing as visions
No contempt extreme coldness
Feels the nature heart in repercussions
We must opposite troublesome cramps
By those exceeding implosive.
Emotionally a speak is not believed
When entombed self-abuse is a life
Of cramming others.
Blessed no contemplate death by
The lovers who couldn't get what they don't
Suffer makes no justice.
Compelling darkness vexatious the soul so all lullaby
Lights can be not anguish to flesh in depth.
The shadow of these is be opposite always
Tongue the eye lips dust the repented

(Merton VIC, 7.00pm Sunday, 2013-07-01)

BY A VIRGIN MAN

Let the virgins have a say,
   Have a right to write.
Let the blues not be far virgins
Centuries many virgins are healed
Not all virgins are boys or girls.
Reduce the age of space to the lands' lovers
Re trench the hurt virgins when the mind is small
   And despair of hearts.
Don't tragic the virgin's path
   Man of mad breeds.
All virgins are poets.
Let no womens say they not
Give the virgin garden of silents
Aloud enough to bring down devils
Of butterflies' talks.
Let the virgin vote the government out of the entirely
Laws they made.
No episode sun shines without a virgin's cry in the rainbow
Of moons of lips.
The sexes of virgins are sacred,
Ashes to lasting always was the virgin earth
But the bodies run human transforms.
By a virgin mans

(Merton VIC, 7.00am, 2013-07-06)

DISBURSE MY VOICE

Nationalism the terror of faceless victims
I am a sniper nice and invader
Strip measure of humanity
I am an autumn lethal eyebrow
I am a courageous turmoil to those,
    Middle skull confusions
No doubt my whether skills
No dilemma of sentence to a brother
    Will twist my violent over capitalist's symptoms.
No enjoy homicide makes my life's spasm
Brutal mercy stays with the arranges
Pencil scribbles are corpses of the new
    Fingers move beyond questions of identity.
The ruthless characters are party to
    Counted snipers no gala cool ho's
Bliss whispered consciences deliver
    A stream of wasted infantrys.
This was at the times of the sniper's
Lovers reader bed concern of the river meet her portrays.
This at times desired highway-blazed flowers to take the impaired eyed.
My penalty came torment for zones where posture tantamount sat.
I am her sniper electric disposition
I orbit the singing cup of galaxy around,
Morning memories over their forbidden.
Tilt coffee and tea in the subways faces,
And you all will find me the SNIPER
BURSING THE VOICES TO THE SNIPERS

(Merton VIC, 8.15pm, 2013-07-06)

MEAN'S LAND NGUTA IN LAUGHTERS

Loneliness is not the poet, orders a poet now?
When the audience likes your socket to them words,
    I am happy in minds
When the audiences are apart of the papers
The pages gave, and then I am a voice
When audiences power the after life write more —
When seduced protesters are country heart
   The beat off a poet is powerfully.
Walk the write sing the write mind it I am the writer,
When the dead reader are written to live
   A word by the Murri writers
Sacrifice our autographed are heard.
When several hands are hitting the ceiling
   For the writers' words are bubble underneath their chairs.
A craft happen on every control thumper of tunes, then the writers
   Have art in string of pictures.
When soft poems are irritated by anger
   Young will find shouts are cornets
When morning meets the poet with sun lit star ring of night number
Of years gone by.
Many neurotic floating sky will question the eyes lip in ears
That drank the mouth's memory.
When people sit with no audiences then remember the poet
Who said land lay in clouds, land cares.
When written words pregnant the captive pastures.

(Merton VIC, 10.00am, 2013-07-08)

HISTORICAL UPHEAVALS

Walk white fellow, as you all can't write
Our battle just at your sunrise and night sigh ties.
The noble note runs in our native modern now from then.
Black resistance is everywhere now on written,
Face books their door mat roof an in-laws.
Walk white fella, you all can't rights us.
First lovers black and loving came and stays
No fables dreams stop our mountain eyes,
Bodies for the dirt tears can't ours, pains can't our pens.
Resistance with us makes no trance but struggle over struggles,
Resent resistance.
The black diligent are our gent, believe it ladies.
We appreciative our fighter of these times
Awaken white vital man physical to a black world women's call.
They'll find renewed upsurges.
Continuing the non-silence is what we about
Lazy exterminator in their policies
Will fall to a decolonisative voices powered by our master race.
Wall up white fella, as your impediments will not combined.
Our men sang weak walk on white fell as meant economic
Are seen to wider our children's fight.
The continent still not there's even in numbers contribution
    historical upheavals
Walk in sleep, walk in lifeless is still,
The dreamer's white man men made

(Merton VIC, 2013-07-06)

BIOLOGICAL BARRIERS

Innocent tranquilizer re bums on pubs
New republic give us the resonate in black red and yellow
    our spiritual
Intellectual for whooshs people and babys.
That capitalism is making your domestic
Conservative to polarize our rights.
The rebellion is now a purchase sanctuary
    Now for squaring momentums.
Those contemporaries in tenser the blazed proliferates,
So poor for the doors to open.
New frustration of the from pluck machines,
Violent minds rejoice adjustment gives pickle in a blonde
    brain excel rods.
Hateful access is the day dead fetter the rich sexual
    freedom's dead rapes.
Wrench is the poor man's that breathe expression of dreadful
    in infidel generation republic a petrified zombies.
Superiority is a weakness that rest for power in lust insecurity.
The people's person pull gravity as impotence to Ultra
    exploited thrown to sociologists pitifully sensations.
Brute bias is administrator productions
They strive to idolize images so we as recognition get scorned.
The great headshrinkers by the elite personifies a remain
    of foredoomed.
New republic crackers are individual level for mass levels…

(To Sister Kirsten Parker, Merton VIC, 9.00pm, 2013-07-08)

KITCHENS OF THE KETCH UPS

I press my words in no mind
    Just their injustices
We evaporate cloths from the 1960s
   So circuits can see how we were naked,
Nails in socks, hawks in jeans, dry sweat in noses.
I swallow the unused nerves for my room's snapping
Bed click go the button shoes up the roof drop dresses.
We stomach a lean on cushioned leg stand up belly beer mans
As his next to slow kiss he gave.
I field the space of the sweaters and skirt of the futures when
    no money was in the snowdrop lines.
We brushed away habits by the marriages who rich acid in
    their trays.
I suicide all my hands to the indistinguishable strange chewed
    ultimate nightmare.
We will manipulate trust of the ungracious as no conversation
    in times as wallpaper.
I murdered the dreaming with a white apron so we can eat in
    the massage soap cupped up stumbling palms.
We no in take vanity of others never given pavement a fragment
    for the rich land as the smell of all cleanest histories.
I press a barber's world for the new hairs to grow we pails of
    suspended bodies minds.

(Merton VIC, 10.30pm, 2013-07-08)

SCENIC MAPS PARTS

TAKE YOUR SMART PHONE AND RUSH
    A MIND TO ARTIST WAYS
TAKE YOUR I PADS AND FIND THE
PATHWAY THE BLACK MEN WALK AND TALKED BEFORE
THE DEVICES CONTENT DEMANDS.
INFATUATE IN DOWNLOAD OF A DREAMTIME REALITY LAYERS.
HAVE ALL RICH CLASSICS ON THOSE BLACK FELLAS KIDS
    WRITERS NOW,
MAN OF BOOKS ON GOINGS.
MAKE THE MOBILES UNITE A MEDIA TO GO TO OUR NEXT
    YEARS RIGHTS FIGHTS.
DO THE FAVOURITE EMERGING REALM OF LITERATURE OF
    EXPERIENCES.
DON'T FIELD THE WIZENED GHOST THAT EMBED FOR MONEY.
TAKE ALL I PADS AND PUT THEM IN THE OUTBACK STARS
    FALLING FOR THE FIRE LIGHTS.

(Merton VIC, 10.44am, 2013-06-10)

SIGNING MY DEATH LION AND HELL

Yes deeds to reef my death
I am dead at my age now,
I am dying fast and not showing
I feeling that the death calls
   Of my heart is stoping my
       Beat to life
I am dead for a death not
    Rich to live on.
The pains comes and goes
   Me eyes are blending
    Me ear hear nothing
      Me mind can't keep up
        To me writings
I go out just to think my
   Sleeping is unresting,
Song don't seams to be
   The dances I once knew.
The wind I nose don't bring
  Bloods to my feets anymore
I need sex in parts of my body,
But I fear death will bring on.
I am dead singing dead
Living in this moment
One thing I know doesn't want a have a white death.
The voices are dead to my worlds.
They say you are KILLING ME,
Bloods show on every level
And my finger is weakling.
My neck turns like fire fly into my knees

To drop as cold in my chest leg to lock on lifeless.
I am die and I don't want know one or people's
To know; come take me now,
Those that mind my stay
Are curled up evils.
Those that sit in judgement are same as the police
Who took us with injustices?
So fuck the who hide their silly ways cause they couldn't LOVES.
Forever the past was present
Forever the present is past.
Only timeless life tells
My back is out of shades
And my smiles to laugh
Are dead to nails in doors.
Tomorrow rain now a wait for dry waters face to hit my death.
Now my prehistoric cave
   No matter where can take I
     My gorgeous works will be
        Kept by the grandchild.
           I intended to die this way
Origin of my own strange ways.
From my waist to the tips of
   My hairs my death will have
       A vision for minds to live happy and brave.
An offering of the spirit is not of my body, but trees
The next death to be not dead.
Playground weaver the birds in my groves.
Teachers will see hear my death
Flames will destroy war to be war at my death.
I am Black Death to the futures,
And I am demolition of death,
Mother has my fears and don't let Fathers fig

My flower of wilts wits.
The painted dead as come for me and a colour is catastrophe
Of my death in spirits.
As written in death so I'll
Not live for those of reviving evils.
My transformed death will not cluster for their stars.
Let my footprint be the blood heart that stoped.
Bugs of winged exist on overflowing my gradually death.
Melody wills explosion my death to the dead now alive.
No plank branches will middle road what I seen in my death.
Screams of limbs evening sky are ready to glitter my dark
    celebrated death.
No imprisoned life will stop this dead thing I have.
Mournful tears are bloods for my death now.
Grasslands destruction are faces I to miserable my poetry.
Awaken not my death peculiar dreams for the lies are far
    beneath the weeping's.
She don't want I ever
Restore my soul to the hole
He don't want I ever
No crossroad wills barren this death fields I have.
Dispersal my body to the peoples of corpse now.
No phony national word gave me life but death.
With my thousand words the dead woods are white dreams.
Whistle the dead calls at morning night and depart away my spirit.
Starless days are able to shine death, as rouse is use for me to die.
Let silence be the cry when I am gone,
Let dreams be forgotten when I am your death,
Listen it's time for me as the writer to die.
Reside my other lives for the heart seeks no more.
Reflect my remain to the death of it all in all.

(Merton VIC, 8.00pm, 2013-06-11)

ALTERNATIVE TRIUMPHS

When each dreams are blessed in favour
Of we almost fall into English pictures.
Black men's love enfolders a pillow sun-kissed
Happier peace of no frenzied flights.
Every man proudly became armed on
Western bulldogs laws as their
Teeth depth the lips to bliss neighbours.
At the aftermath time came boiling past
By past, they a brushed branch became
Dreamy whispering unhurt whirling
Voice in leagues for the blue black
Inherited doubtful names.
Famished reaching fire rivers found
An underside humid love so ghastly naked.
Yet this gave life to the skeleton of our dead,
In the overhung waste some in Australia was laughter
By flooding half-mast responsive.
These days' academics absorb more black fellas to recruitment
To their systems.
No substitute for the rationalize souls,
When each feeble restoration came to be affiliated, most trustees
Became external personal protesting.
Forever pictures by English failed.
Australia is behind the styles
Australia can be in our styles
Now conventional experimental are candidates.

(Merton VIC, 8.30am, 2013-06-13)

EDIT NO STORY

Love in death never rest in the life,
When bad vibes are grave dusts to blame others.
Laws in death are as true to life as the
   Struggle to live air in all mouths.
Many a morning sun rainbows show darkness
As a light for night stars are under grounds.
Life run means feets must be food of the
Arms where legs holds all bodies as one.
No time bring peace, yet peace as to have times.
The blow of fire bring all coals an images
The below of a tree as roots yet dirt hidden
On the leave makes the water of morning to earths.
When good baby cry this as songs written
   Before the writers speaks.
When parents drink firewaters restless is at play.
May we art without money or pens
   To make the paint not pain eyes into says of what's that lips hears.
The space of in the city family pace up and down the streets forever.
They look wall to walls, as roofs are needs for the next storms.
Chain no memory where sea meets the men who first kissed.
Chain a saving where banks are withdrawn
By the rich well off poor definitive.
An end to stories is death by reader of the books given by revolution.
Letters to the dented are to be spiritual pass overs.

(Merton VIC, 2013-06-14)

SURGICAL MOILS

Songs that sang
Ends by the drops of rain
Sentinel singing raped the faces,
So sad on the city walk ways.

Songs written bleeds a bark
  Paint perch lip as words.
A speaker's neck uphold the tone
    Said when no words tourer.
No power needs protection,
When freedom feathers the importance to chant.
Motion are the Poet, who worn once
   The people's fight when they could not action.
The song sang by our wishers
   Of peace and unity gave laughter
      Many times over injustices.
Empty ebony fades the ignoring,
Till an impulsively danger of a waring
   The gear of hope to the puppets.
Singing the hits by blackfellas
  Back to future new songs.
We ship those slipping suspense
To the children's taste on tongues.
While now wind wild harmed no remainder tempos.
Interconnected elegantly eyes coveys a desire
For the song man to song the women's
  Songs unsung

(Merton VIC, 5.00pm, 2013-06-20)

1788 TO THE GATES OF 2028s

Whitewash as another history now.
Mythical voices are vast an empty
   In the society's states.
Commission fails all people's pamphlet
     Wrap truths
Internationalists are an alternative for us natives custodies.
Time includes love's confront on every
   Theme's reviews of this antithesis.
The revised Medicare main stream
   Projects are now blackfellas madness.
They conquered brave noble men with
   Ingenious hardworking ideologies.
Mean they are those dominions who
   Have jubilee event by the obligations.
Cannot section us no more.
The collapses of consequences give us
Forcing rise over governmental continents.
Black wash Capitalist to wear our,
"Bodies souls" and valuing stock market,
So parliament stuffs us a west minster babies.
Sacred sites are the first sights.
No complex mind now, but spread over lives corroborees.
My and your mythical are real to the facts of wealth in all there,
Private new worlds orders.
Has history another places, we'll see OK.

(Merton VIC, 8.00pm, 2013-06-21)

FEDERATION STILL LIED

We have been seen like this before
   Clumsy flint to make powers by our ways.
Restaurant rant where we sit, just to eaten,
    Soup seated superficialities.
The marauders of missiles are numbered to fire
They before have heard us, by laws.
Devoiced intelligence chapels sentences,
Principal distinctions on how we speak
   Now write even art.
Verdict besieged many a natives, suring brains.
Academic whipped by their own sufferings
Scholar spell test perfect emotion in stirred primitives.
We bridged this clash wank station
    When colours are placed by prize.
Temporarily property revolutionary are destitute while.
Hospital mouthed flavoured checks,
   Eyes of oasis touched geological words.
Past aspect are play out foul mission brims
Boundaries where basin springs recharged,
  Gave pastoral highlanders to the flat-lines life's treasons.
Master tribal blacks still brake objectionable.
We rich peoples are relies on wildlife's
   Treasures now.
The poor peoples are centimetres of pipe work planted alones.
Wisdom burrows table dugout scrub lovers in alignments.
We had these before, now this is the now.
FEDERATION STILL WANTS YOUR VOTES TO LIE

(Merton VIC, 4.00pm, 2013-06-22)

IMPOUNDED BLACKLISTS

Atheism is stigma by religions,
That pragmatic the fakers.
The delinquency of justice
Was the problem since models?
Didn't work, for the elders employ.
Rebellious initial recoiled the characterized,
Youths at the times seasons changed patterns.
Bloodthirsty eyes watched how hands moved injustices,
For money stages.
Misfits haircut their face lines
   Just to fit in authority.
Now self-image attitudes give imperial centuries,
Of minds over tolerances.
The delinquency arch-villain
Principles of the established subordination to rhetoric,
Inculcated matter races.
   The requisites smile with those prides a manifest,
      Destiny so exploitation.
When victorious supremacy repressive consciousness
Lay around justice to injustices many are impounded
   And left blacklists eating atheism for the stigma by all religions.

(Merton VIC, 5.00pm, 2013-06-23)

ORAL THIS TRANSCRIPTS

Pride happy were pound life lives
Happy seeing laughs real,
   Songs made no wrongs.
Happy joy over doors rated
   Seas open the bush water faces.
Happy when sad saves death,
   Life run beds laughable.
Happy the birth as lives,
   A shouted caller,
Silences please wise passage in all times.
Happy your dance sits on ways unknown,
Now leg all same, hands the hands.
Happy the smile that didn't laugh.
Flower seeded a tree of happiness
Happy the mind made a poet fight lost causes,
Of cosy pain are gone write an arts.
Happy no one when the tired ate rice,
For earth rights because the life longs.
Happy peace unity gave a lip passion kisses.

(Merton VIC, 6.30pm, 2013-06-23)

ENVY PUDDLES

Ugliness galaxy a battle not seen,
   Question fleeing grains of feelings.
They were travelling a destination to me,
When heart stopped pumps made arts,
When art was to be poetry.
Drawing was lost for painter's times,
They were the dead that lived a life.
Walked ran seeped for sands are the worlds.
On earth with pages in reasons.
Sun wind airing the hold hot colds.
Now captured knowledge flew,
People on people without names.
Drafts so countable we had to rest at the fires not lit.
Envy mud's puddles fallen by read roadsides.
Infinity came the unity as naive nice fluttered monsoon,
   Exquisite women wanted a poet's sad lover affairs.
They are the life of millions, extinguished by a morning,
Childhood's bouquet of abandoned.
She travels a written un-poetry,
   Just before the writer said this is what,
I want to dim poets,
They were heart travelling by the poets' hearts

(Merton VIC, 7.30pm, 2013-06-23)

NO CLASSES

Nomads are gone the nobler
 Reach desert spaces are city
  Scorched tyrants' crowns.
No more jobs for lands or communities.
No man theft the new government
 For we are too embittered our money,
  Stern to the futures.
Sums on lust some struggle harder.
Acute general store holds now foods
Pride of how we eat.
Even how we speak to sleep.
Cute crippled dormant scraps for jobs
 In depends of half a note.
Sold by wants, now allotment,
Fancy possessive float run the streets
 Once were lands.
Nomad once roamed free with the keys.
Ashes of traitor and informer bring
Cigarettes beer slink by doors of gutless careers.
Tolerate were lived if poor if rich.
Medicate damper mind cash in your face made,
Appointed offices.
The semi-government needs promises
To bow-out employed noble substance,
People's voiced markets.

(Merton VIC, 7.45pm, 2013-06-25)

ANONYMOUS ARE OUT NUMBERED

Work is the hands of toes behinds
   Purse those hearts warm in lucks
Strength the poor stability as splendour
     For firmness of life's
Light in dark eyes of black red yellow
  Gives certain sunlights, when windows are closed.
Pride our thrills in praise, as our beat is glory higher.
All rivers still will make,
     Friends richest in warm
        Morning soft as fields special
         Fall on night stars wind,
           Covering the all countrysides.
Work the work was done can work.
Troubled by complete dreams not true in lasting.
Fortune cheers most ambition,
  As happiness stand the dead of all-dead.
Gladly life pathways health to enjoy,
     A lead people's new years.
Hand the art of hearts
Let tears sends sad wishing to hell.

(Merton VIC, 2013-06-26)

TRAVEL A FLY OF NO RETURN

On this weekend stay cool
   On this week stay loosely
      On this New Year stay ready to write
Over the hard heart make land the money
   Over there asking stay to myself
      When he calls, keep all those I have
         Gave a new poem
On the rest, make our walks speak
   The things we never done.
On lovers' mornings, let the love
     Be nigh ties fallings
On a summer day let cold feets
   Be beneath our lips
Don't trust one's rusting the painters
     First eyes open over the weeks ahead.
Fly paces with times bodies veils
Fly ace as cards can be for us
Fly life where no one sits, but lay
   Ready on every detail.
On the weekend don't let overseas
   Thoughts stop your present
     Over seeing things so big on the wheels of change,
   "Take the road"
Now your age, seems real for next weeks,
     Bed times reading show alike.

(Melbourne airport VIC, 9.00am, 2013-06-28)

CURRENT LIFE DRESS MAKER

He cherishes her borderlines
She was hung up on a prayer
As groove remembers word polygon the sex.
The brain was strained for sequences
Aboriginal economist became an advocacy
   For bachelor mens who had wives?
He was the computer
She is the technology
As humanities looked for honours
Lot of degree fell in LOVE with social legal accountings.
She is enabling his diploma by going to bed together.
Early education gave software
   For the carminative pant to get a practitioner.
But masters in poems, when online just to range PhD programs.
You all see the commitment was deep passion flexible develop
The tertiary if not for the adult.
Freedom become the next life's,
Business is now journey talents.
Current on the life's dressmakers.

(Melbourne airport VIC, 9.30am, 2013-06-28)

CAUSED US TO BE COLLABORATOR

Their minds in times is what rhymes
We see their words beyond any acceptable meaning
And this is how we express their Dreaming

Because a Black man woman cool done it,
    For all first and human.
Written on paper for the poorest
Wrote on bark for the richest
Because International 1920 Minjerriba she's readopted.
Because intentional Wiradjuri mind he educator,
  Of body's pains for spirit higher educating.
A poetic kill of those non protest writers,
Even oiling the dramatist idea after death to the up coming.
Because this woman man contributing never fades,
A house in his name must be given as foundations abilities.
Never we pay injustices by his words,
We say the price of patriot's lives out of the pages he gave, as
    he's legend.
Australians needs to know, survival by Black writers who talk
    read in the pickers' sovereignty hits the heart to love the
    minds to fight rich bug gars of edged level demands.
The healing of national treasures,
Don't stay on the fringes.
So people's poets think for his positive process.
So main man Mr Gilbert is the messages for our baby's writer's
    cultural matrix.
Streams of influence are seen read in those who don't know the
    black man woman writing even when it touches when not
    there hey?

Because ghosts are not alive, but the voice off the paper
 reconciliation our negotiation to answers.
Foisted simply power giving us intelligentsia,
Who can galvanisation the call to political actions?
Repetition of the majority written forms is broken by
 provided powers.
Because the white man cannot write, means he's cannot speak
 for the introduce Black from jails.
Let alone repeat the forces of how we must write.
Here Mr Gilbert boarded all our widespread solutions.
Only if they have listen to him may he would be dead or alive.
Treaty reference is legislative frames in occurred lifetime position.
Yet the necessary times declare of plague in the affairs are
 indigenous condemnation of their dimension writers.
Being the playwright's solitary vision gave us aspirate facts to
 give criticism of Governments present.
Strike appeal intervened epilogue in no debate but outcomes
 and say just because he absence is ours to rethink refight
 and rewrite.
I witness this great venom,
I withstand this great vernacular,
  The kind of fashion glorious of our prides.
Liberating words where we have half the times don't need words.
A resists on evil by enshrines of poems so immortal that's all
 our legendary never needs to keep on quest justice, but to
 live its determination without convictions.
The dictum by those written dead poets are to oppress terror
 by the white man's laws.
Personal becomes echo of authentic grass-roots politeness,
Still shows to have peace must protest
Still shows to have apology must not lay down our dead who
 fought for the refusals still our peoples do.

I witness spiritual reflect of great experiences in they are apart of all our ultimately writer fighters even lovers of the sentences to go on forever.
Perform our unions to instil Aboriginal in years to come still greater authors,
Oodgeroo Noonuccal, Mr Gilbert.
He and she had a white side,
Knowing get their words out to clean up the untrue written poetry of politics.
They lived near white foe but never stole their ideas or rid to get rips.
They were common but differ in how to pawn the way over and around the Miggloo brains.
They even had a good go at their own kinds.
Anyways every out massacres to lectures was to shame the systems and make human righties loves be a thing of essential.
The original most in heartlands cannot be a new Australian spirits for the original made us richer on the steel worlds forecasts.
Now new ones hype on their medias communicate for that magic formulate.
So just because we will never change the way they wrote, we can learn look and sit for the teachings.
Please Ooodgeroo Noonuccal and Mr Kevin Gilbert pregnant us again,
I all in all dawns of the night's day's writer's futures.
Because us writers arts can do it all for all thanks and thanks again
Call us the collaborators of their books.......

(Anywhere, 2013-06-29)

SAINTS ARE HOMELESS

The poor not homeless cause they have souls richest.
Fortune are homeless, tunes are homeless,
Homeless be the resistances
Homing babies don't cry
Homeless be the rich of explores
Renting and owners be a homeless
Souls of cold are homeless
Soulful houses are hot with that foods want by the homeless.
Now prayers don't work for homeless
A camp tent disappear, when a house no tiles to walk on.
Beds all lay sensible as inflict a strategy by all homeless survival.
Resistance are many homeless when they are exhibited.
Homage strange ungirth bring sad eyes handled by transgressor.
Love can not be a molesting, "we got it better to live"
Home made invader on our homeless are tears not seen to
    comfort the living.
Home sweet homes must look at the big pictures.
Poor fairest bring all your morning happy when rhythms are
    lullaby as if the house is earth.
Home swear will not cover the hot cold seasons our
    homeless needs.
Religions are using the unhoused people for forgotten
    bush realization.
Pain comes passion at the men who needs a home to home
    his women.
Society eternity seems to want a keep homeless at bay at no stay.
Gifts are given, yet the homeless can't pay rent or play ownership
    no more at doors gates close, a whole history roofs side walls
    seems fallen by the homeless callings.

My people housed know they not full housed cause our people's
   live air think even eat as homeless.
Land taken made us homeless.
The trees roots are arms of our brothers and sisters homeless.
They say why don't them get it together.
Well knock pale the rising sun light on homeless.
We'll find music is beat best in homeless songs.
Always not be homeless for the crowd will intake,
Swift perfect lives make no homeless we run through years of rain
   in the sun shining.
Their feeling are not homeless when not housed don't mean they lost.
Homes many are lonely than the homeless song on songs.
Let the peace be the piss over fires that don't warm the homeless kinds.
The golds are the homeless
The futures are all homeless
Just don't be up you ones of a housed care.
Don't cares are right wing bad bodies mouths.
We pity the stay on owners who will not house the homeless.
Most homeless have peaces unity and loves over money wearing
   sparkling.
Most homeless do soul the soulless even smart talk the politic of it all.
Most homeless are friends without friends.
We must not feel sadden for the homeless are a real worlds.

(Merton VIC, 8.30am, 2013-07-02)

DECEIVED THE AUTHOR

The fantasy came when the romance
   Was to being paranormal.
Now scary evocative love
   Got re-imaged
A beautiful attributed dressed fashion
   Woman gave a man adopted feelings.
But the encapsulate genre became the hype of others.
No companion was the man,
So she lapped her scenes.
No common interchangeable approach
   Made the classes authors.
Confusion is the readers as the audience became
   Glamorous in designees.
A big criss-crossed position was now shelfs for words.
Mode in proven corset gave expression faraway wistful surveys.
The realist were billowing backdrop blacks,
As enchantment too identify.
Deceived the authors.

(Merton VIC, 2.30pm, 2013-07-03)

TIMES OFF HARD LOVERS

All the womens I lusted for dust,
    I am not your rust or hurts.
Now I am free over souls on seas,
All the womens who gave me,
A baby they'll become men and women
    And know me more over.
All the pains I had are in all the plains and plane,
    Is now placement of my hearts?
Live the times of caring magic.
All the sex I had now is my state to later.
Rest in peace feed the tests.
To those eyes that balled my eyes for sad return,
Not going to happen again, justice sized by times.
To happy air I smelled my body is wanted.
All the womens said they knew me was not,
Sew your lips cause they never kissed.

(Merton VIC, 2013-07-03)

RESEMBLED LOYALTY'S

        Underestimation were the lovers,
           Of the explorers.
     These are blankets and sugar
        Tea flour lectures of dangers.
    These are tact track over that expedition
      Who treacherous overwhelmed us natives?
        Time caused inferiority in numbers now observed.
          Naively the battle was to attack Aborigines futures.
             Yet nervous apprehension runs in lot of casualties.
Today ringleaders confine few to speak on radicalization.
Tonight irresponsible is the state as industry reveals protector,
  Of the rich gives feuds and disputes.
     Backed by pastoralist were the ones punitive to profits.
       Ruined and awaken by reserved enticing no lovers
         Policy was underestimation.

(Merton VIC, 10.00am, 2013-07-04)

REPETITION SOLITARY DAD WHERE'S MUM

Witness prides of venom, and liberate glorious.
Sign a song for hate be no more,
Sing countries not known
Sing a just season where winds
    Are forever smiles where tears are joy.
Song the leaves fallen by life's alive.
Eat a food off the rich trees,
    For the poor breads us all.
House the sad, but be glad on releases.
    Sing up lived wishes to come truth,
Song along roads alone.
Stay with all children's loves
    When mums have done.
Stay with all children's loves
    When no dad as rights.
For the songs are mums and dad when not there.
Sign peace in the unity hands making legs arms,
Apart of the earth's flowers.
Sang are those dances in eyes to eyes seeing,
Feets moving to present sounds.
Justice a word every air where change stay same.
Paint all songs without the moving of lips,
Then touch feelings passion unseen.
Repetition the solitary Dad where's Mum

(Merton VIC, 9.00pm, 2013-07-04)

BORRI IS FIRE WARU IS FIRE

Fire is our right
Fire OH fires our lives
We had no cooked food, fire was there.
Time needs fire, rain needs fire
Sky eyes had to have sun's fires.
Winds were and are friends to fires.
The fire can kill, when not looked after,
Safe by fire makes new peoples a unity
Fire made not by man but natures
Can't stop old fire
Can't stop young fire
Open fire warm earths all bodies
In heat fire is wanted for without the cold were.
You and we are without age-old fires.
The belly guts ribs fires on the lip fire speak sings to the ears.
Fire brings sex rest and cares
Aboriginal's fires are power over laws
When it love brake homeward.
These fires are under ground waiting for house
That disrespect man using.
So beware fire as luggages and fatly takes lives in speeds.
Colour is fires over dark light rainbow show fires are signs.
The trees never grow without fires.
Every bodies needs fires to creator song,
To dance walk stand fires have places.
In the valley mountain dark fires don't lie.
In all morning fire await wood fallen from the trees of fires
    birds fireflys.
At night to see space fires are wanted

At stars fire plays eyes to the blind.
Fire is unity when care is peace for the blanket of beds the fire gives.
Fire gives all written painted artist what we have now animals fires.
If there's no fire, earth dead and the world will be misunderstand
Fire on fire to put out fires.
The city be nothing without fires
The countries be nothing without fires
Our roads when made needs fires
Fires is the stories log and bush
Fire lay every birth for humans
All fire thrown still the wars sweet evils are fires of wronged.
Sweet heaven dreams fires to get away from evils.
Dreaming using love fires finds ways to bring together kindest.
Many thing are said for fire, all season around fire arms all babies restless
Dreaming is fire for babies.
Many pretty fires close the gabs off sad tears, as waters are the real loves of fires
Waters are nothing without fire,
Fire burns under waters.
Ready is fires on anytimes.
Humanities are fire
My race is fire
The spirit is fire
We use fires spirits to heal
Being in side fire the grass growth
As green round of joy smiles when fire rising.
The moon cherish the fires
The sun still needs our fires a blazing below.
To have vision fires are important
To have schools fires is education
Much death as fires for a life

Much life as fires for a death
Let the house of fire live for happy livings.
Love of fires is the fight
Fire of lovers is to take it easy
Friends are fire Brother with care
Friends are fire Sisters with stares
Don't fire out the fire made a Thousand years ago.
For the stories are kept by these fire stories.
Fire now is the book of face fires.
Fire runs men's and women's in every work they do.
No poetry is alive without fire,
Words are fires written for action.
All poet stand as fire, No one is poet without fires.
Fires are the hearts for fire bloods,
Dry creek beds cry for fire from the sea fires to unite clouds abodes.
The creator made us fire for our well beings.
The future will always say fires will state again for seeds are
    sprang by fires.
Waru Borri walk
Waru Borri talks
Waru Borri our eyes
Waru Borri dances us nice
Waru Borri loves the lovers
Waru Borri can hate
Waru Borri can kill
Waru Borri live for death
Waru Borri can rainbow your days
Borri sits even as wits in lit
Let the stars shone bright bellow our sleep the Waru Borri
    will be safe.
Let the control off the fires be always man's
    Knowing its powers

No wars must be fires
No personal baldest be fires
Oh he got the fire in his speak let it be of greater peace
If to write be to fight, do it with fire better and right with the good campfires stories.
Ghosts are fire death in tales
Ghosts knows fire, but are not creator of fires.
Be the Waru Borri of fire in sighs to riot stone
For tomorrow we needs still fires

(Merton VIC, 2013-07-05-6)

MERCY A MEMORY

At the future childs are
To grow with wise words.
Hide lie when truth beds tomorrows.
At the past child no need live,
Unless wisdom for gave.
In past history was who push the rights,
In the Mothers' love respect cannot be given,
When troubles are shout shows.
In the Fathers' love of respects,
Unity seeds the growth.
Button finger are numbered.
Man alone as times of all spaces and return,
Peace into not fights.
Yo no love no respects given word.
Women teaser of sex makes eyes lie
And ear blocked by small yarns.
Now children's love to love is passion,
By swinging the rivers of non-evils.
Contemporary committee are to beware,
Of apart must be fullest.

(Merton VIC, 3.30pm, 2013-07-07)

BEFORE THEY SAID HITS

I got your respects sitting here
I got love lying in your lover here
I got lone stars at the nesting here
I got minds of poets' mirroring me here
I got fights ready for any 26 junta all night long
I gotten for get me nots around this city subs
I got all countries in my body bust in bushes
I git to speak for the unwritten not a face bull list's
I got hate still to the Pigs of powers
I got hanging thoughts of capitalist placements
I got hornet honest off people's loves
I am the Man of your words be for you said it's ok
Before they cane us we are the men and women
Voice of the reconciliation papers has negotiation
    is a political actions.

(Merton VIC, 4.00pm, 2013-07-07)

CONCENTRIC BLACKS FLEETS

Curiosity came to my dreams
   As tongues endangered justices
   Be it was over a peoples.
Dreaming where no people
   Were abused, shared tears were rides.
Murdered by power passions abbreviation
Pour out cleanses.
The fate of my poetry bow a hold,
A whispering stream enters my system gloomy,
Yet a survivor's whirl embroils many pleasures of harmony.
Equal alienation whistles were natural married curiosity.
This change made strangers stretch views on the images
By the window of dead birds, an epic materialized.
Chilling erect dreams was now my greasy life gets up morning,
Calm a present.
Curiosity was now satisfaction just when I wanted to kill,
A mess smoked city.
My feeling changed to concentric fleets.

(Merton VIC, 5.00pm, 2013-07-07)

ANTHOLOGY OUR INTERNATIONAL

The International needs us now Black Red Gold

   Wars over worries gone.
Our International loves need us
   On every unity walk for the talks.
Here on earth all people are personal to one's rights.
Yet the community wants are rich to rich for the poor's.
The International causes are same as the days ahead.
The night differ yet the bloods feels same as cuts
Are put in to arms to cover the stars under our all feets.
We have International kisses for the not so lovers.
Pain stay here as rains of suffering leads help
   By the cost of life full.
Let the human women take us men to spaces
Open with the dreaming stories for all International worlds.
He International, Her national leaves
Now those entire anthologies are our International's

(Merton VIC, 8.30pm, 2013-07-07)

NON-PAIN IN RAIN

No matter who lands?
Earths our same lands
Matter what worlds depend
    On cost and prices.
No matter whose blood we
Feed the same mouths.
Matter what love, for most are lost
With sad out comes.
No matter whose the mobs loses will find the sobs.
New music seeds flowers
Oh but words needs the matter.
Land matter to every ones when done own it.
Heart pump the land where sky are in the bodies we carried.
Tears are reefs where the sea matter more,
Too feat waters we drink.
No matter who mad, the land will care to relive a matter

(Merton VIC, 9.00pm, 2013-07-07)

"PLANNING WITH MY FLIGHT..."

Planning with my flight
Light my dark man ways
Homeland is the saints not missions
Transport needily is in necessary
Housing to stay in house needs jobs
Work by art happens by souls not sold
Planning a birth beans as it done
Yet where to air in tighten tongues
Fighting raw at doors closed were the rooms
Time clocked by get up morning await the night
Rest nest test all right when wrong are docked
The ride in life shows the sweet sweet lung as care off,
The light turn off on when our sunset lettings by growth
Home alone zones tones ton under grounds above eyes
We sit we lit space black matter for emery
They listen voices past lonely yet lovely.
You read the lines, yet some vines unwise
Made us inclines
Planning around white on the sand dust
Pain down young man, spots is common lands
Paid by layabout seems dead tree greens the root
Home sane taken bush brains stay sane were we lane.
Lighting wind cold sang morning's peace voices to the nations.
Paradise rises in the east for west to lip south so our north can unite untied rights.
No home land man found men same as,
No culture turrets to present speak in all languages
Many heat hearts taken grounds above ace money evils.
The words are mine, now you're for worlds to share

Cooking up food higher for poor to open plains,
Neither planning with my flight hum not death nor
    giving your dead,
Lives are the homelands.

(Fibs on the train in Victoria, 9.00pm, 2013-09-10)

VOTE NO? HO

Remember 200 thousand dreams and the minds balance houses.
    Earth in focus world words around.
Remember to tree in year 3 thousand dreams,
Member those light in side cells life's death
But always be happy over horror in ways.
Remember day one was no big bang
    But sprang water fire wind.
Remember 2030 will be still dirty
    Road open roads close.
Wise thoughts made real dreams path and raft.
Remember a time city lays tin hut and sharing was one on one another.
Remember protest of glass wearing sore eye spoke persons
They just made it bad on bad.
Remember black men's being fat off the sea land.
Remember red blood flow the skin veins
Remember yellow high at every moon's daze,
Up hole young even old when pure histories are tooled,
Up hold needs over wants skinned by ants
Foreseen are cold weathers morning on hot night ties
    Covers by nature's dressings.
Remember been there done was sometimes
    Fun smiling at pains enduring.
Yet 200 thousand smile laughs those odder kind
Away where seeds lift flowers on earth
    Never returning flames.
Remember the black nights turned white no lights just colour remembers.
Remember the smell dreams of futures
History is importance
Home me those past of rich remembers.

(Brisk QLD, 2013-12)

NOTES

PP.9—10: *Bompi*–like a waterfall hitting on your face, the name of a waterfall; *Jackie Joe*–a ridicule name for a black tracker, police employee; Goori–identity term for NSW/southern QLD; Murri– identity term for NSW/QLD; *boong*–derogatory term for Aboriginal people; *Daran*–evil magic.

PP.15—16: *bam gayandi*–changes to the smoke in a smoking ceremony; *dilli*–eyes; *Blount*–a sheet; *jarjums*–children, kids; *gammon*–lie or fibs; *Ngundarui*–the Creator is resting; Koori–identity term for NSW/VIC; *Bam*–changes.

PP.17—19: Noongar–identity term for WA; *Abos*–a derogatory term for Aboriginal people.

P.75: *Nuka*–shells.

P.78: *Yaburuhma*–do always.

P.82: *Nguta*–the country, the land.

PP.102—104: 1920 Minjerriba–the Aboriginal name for Stradbroke Island, home of the Quandamooka people; Wiradjuri–nation tribe of NSW region; *Miggloo*–GHOST people.

PP.111—114: *Waru Borri*–fire and fire; *gabs*–talks a lot, gossip.

Also available from Vagabond Press

Lionel Fogarty, *Mogwie Idan: Stories of the land*

Shortlisted for the 2014 Victorian Premier's Literary Award for Indigenous Writing.

Lionel Fogarty is Australia's foremost experimental and political poet. *Mogwie Idan: Stories of the land* brings together work from across Fogarty's career, including poems from the 2012 Scanlon Award-winning *Connection Requital*, which the judges noted "demands that you move out of your comfort zone and encounter, grapple with, and be open to, the power of his words and the way they are placed on the page and the way their rhythms embody the knotty issues you are being pressed to countenance, accommodate and if possible resolve – or at least come to terms with somewhere in your psyche. This is no easy ride – and Fogarty takes no prisoners."

Mogwie Idan: Stories of the land showcases the intelligence of the Aboriginal grassroots struggle in contemporary Australia, laying open the realness of Lionel Fogarty's Murri mission poetry. The Aboriginal struggle in Australia is not over, but here handed to the next generations to promote their strength. Biame guide! Biame bless!

"A most prolific Aboriginal poet, Lionel Fogarty continues to write with powerful passion about issues close to his heart: injustice, land rights, identity, language, black deaths in custody and the ongoing consequences of colonization. Lionel's writing focuses on his need to face a future without oppression and he demonstrates a desire to pass on his own knowledge and experience through the written word." Anita Heiss

160pp. 2012. ISBN 978-1-922181-02-2

Also available from Vagabond Press

Ali Cobby Eckermann, *Love dreaming & other poems*

In *Love dreaming & other poems* Cobby Eckermann bears witness to a deep commitment to her traditional kin, culture and language as she tells the story of her search for her family on the traditional Yankunytjatjara and Kokatha lands in the north west of South Australia. At the same time, she lays bare the ongoing effects of governmental policy and paternalism on Australia's indigenous peoples. Engaging with events around Alice Springs, these poems give firsthand witness to the 2007 Northern Territory Emergency Response by the Federal Government, commonly known as The Intervention, and its ongoing effects on regional and remote Indigenous communities. These poems lay open the complexity of the internal conflict felt among Aboriginal people today, as they constantly need to adjust to contemporary Australia.

Cobby Eckermann notes, "My times in the desert are my happiest, and the soft blanket felt when my traditional language is spoken around me, is a feeling of pure love." This is a collection by one of Indigenous Australian poetry's most vital new voices, sung with two eyes wide open to the present reality without fear or prejudice, with an overflowing love and care for the future.

"These are the offerings of a writer who has journeyed with great determination through apparently irretrievable loss, through chaos, disintegration and desolation, who has harvested the gifts of insight and emotional and spiritual intelligence and compassion, and who now reveals these insights to the eyes and ears of others through lucid images and punchy language."

Terry Whitebeach

64pp.2012. ISBN 978-1-922181-05-3

Printed in the USA
CPSIA information can be obtained
at www.ICGtesting.com
LVHW092346041023
759905LV00005B/1040